LIFE
fun-tastic

By Andy Economides

Published by **SOTERIA TRUST**

ISBN 0-9541452-0-8

Published by SOTERIA TRUST
PO BOX 103 CHICHESTER PO19 2XY UK

DEDICATION

I dedicate this book to Diane Patry - a friend who made a significant difference.

ACKNOWLEDGEMENTS

First and foremost my heartfelt thanks to my wife Annette for your love and our togetherness in Christ. You are my helpmate and dearest friend. I love you. To my daughter Hannah - I am proud of you.

To Soteria Associates - Phil Dowding, Don Egan and Ian Wilson - Thank you for your brotherly friendship and partnership in the greatest adventure on earth.

I would like to acknowledge the faithfulness and assistance of my trustees, Robin Kemp, Michael Mellows and Derek Mumford. Also to a real and dear friend since our teenage years, J. John.

Thank you to Rev Samuel Folahan, respected by others, respectful of others, like a prince amongst his people.

I would also like to thank Doris Manly, a faithful soldier for Christ, for your encouragement in our work.

A special thank you to the friends and supporters of Soteria Trust who enable us to share the Good News of Christ Jesus in Britain and other counties. You make a difference too.

CONTENTS

Acknowledgements

1. Knowing Christ   7

2. Spiritual Growth   19

3. Peace and Power   25

4. Making a Difference   33

    About the Author

Chapter 1
KNOWING CHRIST

A day that changed his world

Maximilian Kolbe, with four of his companions, was deported to Auschwitz, Poland. Auschwitz was a labour and death camp. Few who passed through the prison gate left the camp alive. Cruelly the prisoners were told that the only way out was through the chimneys of the crematorium. Father Maximilian Kolbe, a Christian minister, received the striped convict garment and was tattooed with the number 16670. He began work immediately, carrying blocks of stone for the construction of a crematorium wall.

Prison Law stated that if anyone attempted to escape ten men from the same bunker would be chosen for death by starvation in the dreaded windowless underground cell. Towards the end of July a prisoner apparently escaped and the men from Kolbe's bunker were led out into the blazing midday sun knowing what to expect.

One man from each line was selected at random, including Sergeant Francis Gajowniczek. The sergeant cried out, 'My wife and children! I shall never see them again!' A man stepped out from the rows and offered to take his place. It was prisoner 16670, Maximilian Kolbe. A German officer asked Kolbe who he was. Kolbe responded, 'I am a Catholic priest. I wish to die for that man. I am old. He has a wife and children.' So it was that Maximilian Kolbe and the nine others were taken to the death chamber of cell 18. Francis Gajowniczek was set free. It was a day that changed his world.

During the next two weeks the prisoners in the death chamber were not given any food or water. One after another they died until only four were left, including Maximilian. The authorities felt that death by starvation was taking too long, and the cell was needed for new victims. Each remaining prisoner was given a lethal injection of carbolic acid (phenol) in the vein of his left arm. Maximilian, with a prayer on his lips gave his arm to his executioner. Maximilian Kolbe was 47 years old when he was executed.

Maximilian's gift of his life reminds me of Jesus Christ's gift of His life for the whole of humanity.

Three years ago during a trip to Poland I visited Auschwitz, which is still surrounded by a triple row of fences which were originally electrified. Inside the prison chamber I stood motionless, gazing through the bars at the dark and gloomy cell in which Kolbe was kept before his death. I could not but think about the amazing love that this one man had for another. Maximilian's act of love was to sacrifice his own life; it was voluntary. This death had purpose - it allowed another, Francis Gajowniczek, to live to a very old age. Maximilian's gift of his life reminds me of Jesus Christ's gift of his life for the whole of humanity.

The day that changed the world

Two thousand years ago something wonderful happened that would affect the world for ever. It was a day that changed the world. Indeed, it was a day that changed history. It was the day God's Son died. God so loved the world that he gave up his one and only Son to be crucified on the cross so that whoever believes in Jesus today may live abundantly - in this and in eternity. Since the day Christ died 2000 years ago until today - and for ever - the cross has never lost its power and effect to forgive, bless, empower and grant eternal life through faith. Jesus Christ took away our sins and sorrows. His death brings us peace of mind and peace with God.

It is important to say that the blood of Jesus is not first

and foremost for us, it is for God. Today God looks upon the finished work of his Son and is satisfied that, for everyone who repents, receives and believes, sin has been paid for.

Millions of people through the centuries have discovered this abundant life and peace with God by responding with faith to the old message. These disciples and followers of Christ have become new creations. The new has come and the old has gone and the world is a different and better place. The church celebrates the day on which Jesus died as 'Good Friday'. The only reason that it was a 'good' Friday was that three days later Jesus rose from the dead - on the day we now call 'Easter Day'.

Jesus Christ's act of love was willingly to lay down his life for humanity for all time. We begin our examination of the events that took place starting at the Garden of Gethsemene the evening before he was crucified. Gethsemene was on the lower slopes of the Mount of Olives just outside Jerusalem, one of Jesus' favourite places.

Overwhelmed with sorrow

Jesus expressed to his dear friends, who had been with him from the beginning of his ministry, his deep distress and trouble. His heart was overwhelmed with sorrow, almost to the point of death. He asked help from his disciples; he needed their friendship, now more than ever. Jesus fell to the ground. He could not help it, because he knew the abuse, suffering, and evil that was to come. He prayed to his heavenly Father, asking that if possible God might take the cup of suffering away from him. But he would rather do God's will, whatever the cost, and therefore acknowledged that he would drink the deadly cup (Mark 14:32-36). While Jesus was talking to his sleepy disciples, Judas the betrayer approached, bringing others with him to arrest Jesus.

Betrayed with a kiss

Judas was aware that people knew Jesus well enough by sight but he felt that in the dim light of the garden they might need a definite indication of who they were to arrest. He chose the most terrible of signs - a kiss. It was customary to greet a rabbi with a kiss; it was a sign of respect and affection for a well-loved teacher. When Judas says, 'The one I kiss is the man,' he uses the word *philein*, which is the ordinary word for kiss. But when it is written that he kissed Jesus, the words used are *kata philein*. The word *kata* indicates intensity. *Kata philein* means to kiss as a lover kisses his beloved. The sign of betrayal was not a mere form of kiss of respectful greeting. It was a lover's kiss. Jesus was betrayed by one of his chosen and closest friends (Mark 14:43-46).

The arresting mob came from the chief priests, the scribes and the elders - the three sections of the Sanhedrin, the Jewish religious council. They marched Jesus away to the high priest. The disciples' nerve cracked. They could not face it. They were afraid that they too would share the fate being prepared for Jesus. They all left him and ran away. But throughout all this Jesus displays serenity, for the struggle in the garden is over, and now there is the peace of a man who knows that he is following the will of God.

Who is Jesus?

The religious trial before Caiaphas, the high priest, was grossly unfair and unlawful. Many people were brought in to tell lies about Jesus, but their statements did not agree and the high priest became exasperated. He asked the question which he knew would get the result he wanted - a sentence of death. *'Are you the Christ, the son of the Blessed One?'* Jesus answered, *'I am.'* That was it. They condemned him worthy of death. The issue here was not about any unlawful deed that Jesus may have done. Jesus never did anything that was unlawful or sinful. They sentenced him to death because of who he claimed to be. He claimed to be the Son of God and the Messiah.

Having passed sentence, they began to spit on him. They blindfolded him and hit him with their fists, taunting him saying, 'Guess who hit you?' The guards also took him and beat him up.

Very early the next morning the chief priests, with the elders, the teachers of the law and the whole Sanhedrin, reached a decision. They bound Jesus, led him away and handed him over to Pilate. He was to be tried by the state now.

Jesus is sentenced to death

Pilate wanted to release Jesus, because he knew that it was out of envy that the chief priests had handed him over. But the continued pressure from the religious leaders and the crowd finally weakened Pilate's resolve to free Jesus. He changed his mind. Now he wanted to satisfy the crowd and he ordered Jesus to be flogged and then crucified.

Roman flogging was a terrible thing. Jesus was stripped naked and tied to the scourging post. The whip had strips of leather studded here and there with pieces of bone and sharpened pieces of lead. The soldiers used this weapon on Christ. His chest, neck, shoulders, back, hips, and legs were slashed as if with knives; his body streamed with blood and was covered with bruises. Even his face was cut and disfigured by the lashes that came down upon him. He was in such a state that he could scarcely have been recognised, even by those who knew him well. Jesus now lay at the foot of the post. A bucket of water mixed with salt was thrown over him, the stinging brine being a routine way to revive a victim and helped to stop the flow of blood. Jesus was pulled to his feet and held upright until he could feel some strength return. His body was racked with pain. Jesus stood shivering in shock and struggling to reclothe himself as best as he could.

The soldiers took Jesus into their headquarters and, calling out the entire company of soldiers, they began to mock him. They dressed him in a purple robe and made a crown of long sharp thorns and rammed it on his head. Then they began to salute him, 'Hail, king of the Jews!'

They beat him on the head with a stick, spat in his face, and dropped to their knees in mock worship. When they were tired of their mocking they took off the purple robe and put his own clothes on him. He was led out to be crucified. The slow walk to Golgotha, the place of the skull, began.

Three soldiers were ordered to complete the execution. The commanding officer took the unusual step of attaching a *centuria*, a further hundred troops in full battle dress, to accompany them. This was a precaution against any attempt to intervene in the proceedings. The procession assembled. First came five rows of soldiers, ten in each row, followed by the execution party made up of three soldiers and Jesus carrying his cross. Then came a further five rows of soldiers, again with ten soldiers in each row. Caiaphas, the high priest, along with the religious guard, walked behind the Roman soldiers and the public followed. There were probably close to four thousand people who went to see Jesus die. The longest way to the place of execution was taken, passing through the business quarter and shopping area. They followed every possible street and lane so that as many people as possible could see and take warning. Jesus, already badly beaten, stumbled under the weight of the heavy cross. A man from Cyrene, in Northern Africa, was close by and they forced him to carry Jesus' cross.

When they reached the place of crucifixion the cross was laid flat on the ground, Jesus was stretched on it and his hands were nailed to the wood. His feet were loosely bound. Between his legs projected a ledge of wood, called a saddle, to take the weight when the cross was raised upright. The cross was then lifted upright and set in its socket. Jesus was left to die. Sometimes prisoners hung for days, suffering hunger and thirst and the terrible struggle to breathe. They offered Jesus drugged wine to ease the pain but he refused it. In the shadow of the cross the soldiers diced for Christ's seamless garment. It was nine o'clock in the morning when they crucified him. Jesus had already suffered so much abuse but it was not over yet. Passers-by ridiculed him. At three o'clock Jesus breathed his last breath. His mission was accomplished (Mark 15:27-39).

... the cross has never lost its power and effect to forgive, bless, empower and grant eternal life, through faith.

As evening approached Joseph of Arimathea, a prominent member of the council, went to Pilate and asked for Jesus' body. Pilate, having received confirmation of Jesus' death, gave permission for Joseph to take the body. Joseph had Jesus' body wrapped in linen and placed in a tomb cut out of rock. A stone was rolled against the entrance of the tomb. Roman soldiers were posted outside the tomb keeping guard. A Roman wax seal was set between the stone door and the entrance. The soldiers had the responsibility to ensure that the seal was not broken. The soldiers guarded the seal with their lives, because Roman law for soldiers stated that allowing a seal to be unlawfully broken was punishable by death.

Christ is risen

Early on the first day of the week, while it was still dark, Mary of Magdala went to the tomb and saw that the stone had been removed from the entrance. So she came running to Simon Peter and the other disciple, the one Jesus loved, and said, 'They have taken the Lord out of the tomb, and we don't know where they have put him!'

So Peter and the other disciple started for the tomb. Both were running, but the other disciple outran Peter and reached the tomb first. He bent over and looked in at the strips of linen lying there but did not go in. Then Simon Peter, who was behind him, arrived and went into the tomb. He saw the strips of linen lying there, as well as the burial cloth that had been around Jesus' head. The cloth was folded up by itself, separate from the linen. Finally the other disciple, who reached the tomb first, also went inside. He saw and believed (John 20:1-8).

One thing is certain: if Jesus had not risen from the dead, we would never have heard of him. The attitude of the women was that they had come to pay their last tribute to a dead man. The attitude of the disciples was that everything had finished in tragedy. By far the best proof of the resurrection is the existence of the Christian church. Nothing else could have changed sad and despairing men and women into people radiant with joy and flaming with courage. The resurrection is the central fact of the whole Christian faith.

The resurrection of Jesus makes Christianity unique

The religious leaders wanted Jesus executed because of who he claimed to be - the Son of God (John 3:16-18). They rightly understood that this claim to be the Son of God meant equality with God. Jesus was claiming to *be* God (John 5:16-19; 10:29-36).

The bodily resurrection of Christ on that first Easter Sunday validates and confirms his claim to be the Son of God. The resurrection also confirms his words and promises to humanity. Jesus spoke of blessings in this life and eternal life in the next. We can be sure of being with God after this life because Jesus promises it, his resurrection makes it believable and possible.

> **Knowing Jesus means experiencing life to the full in this life and the next. Jesus came for that purpose.**

Because we believe in the resurrection something important follows. Jesus is a living presence not just a person in a book. It is not enough to know the story of Jesus. We may begin that way but we move on to meeting him. The Christian life is not the life of a person who knows about Jesus, but the life of a person who knows him. There is all the difference in the world between knowing about a person and knowing a person. Most people know about the President of the United States of America, but few actually know him. The resurrection of Jesus makes Christianity unique. There is no one like Jesus Christ - he is unequalled, unusual and remarkable. Knowing Jesus means experiencing life to the full in this world and the next. Jesus came for that purpose. Know Jesus - know life! No Jesus - no life!

Jesus' death has purpose

Jesus Christ gave up his life willingly. He allowed his life to be taken. He was in control, although the people responsible for his death thought that they were.

While Jesus hung on the cross he cried out those incredible words, 'It is finished!' He immediately breathed his last, gave up his spirit and died. It was a cry of victory: 'I have done it!' He accomplished his ultimate purpose when visiting our world, that of shedding his blood on the cross for the forgiveness of our sin and to bring us to God. We no longer have to be separated from God who is holy and without sin. Separation means no real communication with God is possible. This separation is like a thick cloud that prevents the warm sun from shining on us. The Bible says:

Surely the arm of the Lord is not too short to save, nor his ear too dull to hear. But your iniquities have separated you from your God; your sins have hidden his face from you, so that he will not hear (Isaiah 59:1-2).

When our sin is removed the way to God is clear and we can be friends with our heavenly Father. The purpose of Christ's cross is to bring you to God by removing your sin. The cross of Christ has never lost its power and purpose. 'For Christ died for sins once for all, the righteous for the unrighteous, to bring you to God' (1 Peter 3:18).

Christ is the way to God. It was for our sins that Christ died. The good and righteous one died for us so that we could come to God. Being brought to God means living in close friendship with God, meeting him and knowing him. That is eternal life. It is knowing God and Jesus Christ. Not knowing about but actually knowing God and his Son, Jesus (John 17:3).

The prophet Isaiah predicted the coming Messiah, or Christ:

But he was pierced for our transgressions, he was crushed for our iniquities; the punishment that bought us peace was upon him, and by his wounds we are healed. We all, like sheep, have gone astray, each of us has turned to his own way; and the Lord has laid on him the iniquity of us all (Isaiah 53:5-6).

On the cross Jesus literally took our transgressions on himself. Transgressions means breaking God's laws. We have all done that. He carried our iniquity. Iniquity is the evil that we have done. He was punished that we may have peace. Peace with God. Peace with ourselves. Jesus' death has purpose.

Firstly you need to repent from sin...
Secondly you must receive Jesus...
Thirdly you need to believe...

You can know forgiveness. You can become a new creation. All of this is done by God. It is his power coming within your life, transforming the rest of your life. The Power being the Holy Spirit coming within you, giving you a spiritual birth. It is being born again by the Holy Spirit.

For this to happen you must do your part and God will certainly do his. Firstly you need to repent from sin, to feel deep sorrow about your sinful actions and resolve not to continue in your old ways that are not according to the teaching of the Bible. This change of mind is a turning from sin and turning to God. If we claim to be without sin, we deceive ourselves, but if we confess our sins to God, he is faithful and just and will forgive us our sins and cleanse us from all unrighteousness (1 John 1:8-9). The Saviour of the world died to bring forgiveness. Embrace the Saviour. You need him. Jesus' death has purpose.

Secondly you must receive Jesus, the Son of God.

> But to all who believed him and accepted him, he gave the right to become children of God. They are reborn! This is not a physical birth resulting from human passion or plan - this rebirth comes from God (John 1:12-13 NLT).

Receive and believe

Receiving Jesus means to welcome him into your life. He wants to come and live within your life by his Spirit. Jesus stands at the door of your life and knocks, waiting for you to open the door and invite him in. He says:

> 'Here I am! I stand at the door and knock. If anyone hears my voice and opens the door, I will come in and eat with him, and he with me' (Revelation 3:20).

To receive Jesus means no longer to live your life without him. It involves receiving his ways and purposes for your life. Receive him gladly as your Lord.

Thirdly, you need to believe that God so loved the world that he gave his only son to be crucified for your sins. It also means believing in God's risen son, Jesus the Saviour. Will you put your trust in the cross of Christ? Will you embrace Christ as your personal Saviour? For those who repent, receive and believe, a miracle happens - they experience the new birth.

Think of Jesus knocking now, asking to come into your life. You want him to come in, or perhaps you want to make sure he has come in. It may help you to say this prayer quietly, thinking carefully what you are saying:

Lord Jesus Christ, I know I have sinned in my thoughts, words and actions. There are so many good things I have not done. There are so many wrong things I have done. I am sorry for my sins and turn from everything I know to be wrong. You gave your life on the cross for me. Gratefully, I give my life back to you. I ask you to come into my life. Come in as my Saviour to cleanse me. Come in as my Lord to control me. Come in as my Friend to be with me. And I will serve you all the remaining years of my life in complete obedience. Amen.

Asking Jesus into your life is the first step - like greeting someone you have just met. Getting to know someone well takes time and effort. It is the same with Jesus. We can get to know Jesus better through the Bible, prayer and the local church. Most importantly God has given us the Holy Spirit. The Holy Spirit is a wonderful person available to you, to help you become like Jesus. The Holy Spirit will comfort, strengthen and guide you.

Chapter 2

SPIRITUAL GROWTH

There is only one requirement for salvation - faith in Jesus Christ. Just believe in him. That is all you need to do. Have you trusted Christ as your Saviour and Lord? If you have, you have salvation. To enable you to move forward towards spiritual maturity, the Lord has given various things to help you: baptism, the church, prayer and the Bible.

Baptism

Whoever knows Christ as their Saviour and Lord can be baptised. Those who believe and have accepted the message of Christ should be baptised. Baptism and believing go together. There are three good reasons for baptism.

First, we should be baptised in obedience to Jesus Christ. Jesus gave the great commission to the church, instructing them to baptise disciples in the name of the Father, the Son and the Holy Spirit (Matthew 28:18-20).

Another reason for baptism is to prepare us to serve Christ. Jesus' baptism prepared him to serve God and others. At the moment Jesus came up out of the water he saw the Spirit of God descending in the form of a dove and a voice said, 'This is my Son, whom I love; with him I am well pleased' (Matthew 3:16-17). After this experience Jesus went out to preach and heal.

Saul, later called Paul, was also baptised, which prepared him to serve. Paul was dramatically converted to Jesus Christ whilst on his journey to Damascus. During this experience he lost his sight. Ananias went to the house where Paul was staying and placed his hands on him. Paul's sight was restored and he was filled with the Holy Spirit. Paul got up and was baptised (Acts 9:1-19). For Jesus and Paul water baptism and being filled with the Holy Spirit came before they began to serve.

**We should be baptised
in obedience to Jesus Christ...
to prepare us to serve Christ...
to demonstrate our faith in Christ.**

The third reason for baptism is to demonstrate our faith in Christ. The person being baptised is identifying themselves as a Christian. The act shows that the person is not ashamed of who they are and their decision to follow Jesus Christ (Mark 8:38).

The meaning of baptism

Baptism is a sign that certain things have happened to the person who has decided to follow Christ. However it is not only an outward sign of an inner reality. At baptism it is an opportunity for God to continue his work of blessing and grace in the life of the believer. At your baptism expect God to fill you with his Spirit and empower you to serve. Expect God to break the power of cancelled sin in areas of your life. In Nigeria I have witnessed people who were baptised in water just days after becoming Christians receiving the baptism in the Holy Spirit and deliverance from evil spirits. Let faith arise for greater things.

Firstly, baptism signifies the washing away sins. Just as water cleanses our bodies so baptism is a sign that our sins have been washed away from us. Paul was told, 'Now what are you waiting for? Get up, be baptised and wash your sins away, calling on his name' (Acts 22:16). If we confess our sins the blood that Jesus shed on the cross forgives and cleanses us.

Secondly, baptism demonstrates the burying of our old life. During baptism the immersing under the water represents what happens when someone dies and is buried in the ground. Baptism represents death of the person's old life and ways (Romans 6:4). The old life has gone. When the person is raised from the water it represents new life. Becoming a Christian is about becoming a new creation, the old has gone and the new has come and all this is from God (2 Corinthians 5:17). Baptism shows this.

Thirdly, baptism is a sign of our receiving the Holy Spirit. Peter told the crowd to turn from sin and be baptised and they would receive the Holy Spirit. Jesus and Paul received the Holy Spirit with power at baptism. Expect to receive God's power at baptism. Baptism in water and baptism in the Holy Spirit are sometimes linked in experience and this shows itself in scripture (1 Corinthians 12:12-13).

And fourthly, baptism is a sign that we have joined the church, the body of Christ. By baptism we are bought into the family of the church. All Christians, whatever nationality and background should be baptised. Baptism should not be restricted to adults of eighteen years and over. There are those who have not reached adulthood who have believed and received Jesus Christ into their lives. These young people should be baptised.

**Early baptism is the biblical way
and the church needs to put
a higher value on it.**

The word 'baptise' means to immerse, plunge or sink. This is why many churches baptise people by completely immersing them in water; baptism was usually done this way in New Testament times and Jesus was baptised in this way in the river Jordan. Today people can be baptised in a church building, in a river, the sea, a swimming pool, or anywhere where there is water.

Give baptism priority

New converts and those who have not been baptised should be baptised immediately. Early baptism helps to strengthen and seal the decision to follow Christ. Early baptism is the biblical way and the church needs to put a higher value on it. God's power is released at baptism.

The Ethiopian official had the Good News of Jesus explained to him by Philip the evangelist (Acts 8:26-40). As they travelled together and talked, the Ethiopian saw some water and said, 'Look, here is some water. Why shouldn't I be baptised?' He ordered the chariot to stop. Then Philip and the Ethiopian official went down to the water and Philip baptised him. We see that when the Ethiopian became a Christian he wanted to be baptised straightaway. What is keeping you from being baptised? What are you waiting for? Ask your church leaders to baptise you.

The church

A few weeks after I became a Christian at the age of seventeen, Andrew Liversidge came to my home. I knew him slightly from school days. He had heard that I had become a committed follower of Jesus Christ and asked if I would like to join the church youth fellowship that he attended. I am so glad that he cared enough to follow up my decision to follow Christ. I started to attend the youth fellowship which met on Saturday and Sunday evenings. Soon I also went to the Wednesday evening meeting which met in the youth leaders home for Bible study, prayer and fellowship. The youth leader, Roger Stacey, became a spiritual father to me. Those early years were vital in my formation and development as a Christian. The love and care that Roger and his wife Kate gave to me was wonderful. They were true shepherds. Later I became one of the leaders of the youth fellowship. It was there that I met a lovely young woman whom I fell in love with and married. During this time I also attended church regularly on Sunday mornings and made friends with other Christians.

I am so glad that he cared enough to follow up my decision to follow Christ.

The Christian needs to attend the fellowship of believers, that is the church. This fellowship is the coming together of people in friendship. In the early church those who heard, believed and accepted the message of Christ spent their time learning from the apostles' teachings, taking part in the fellowship, sharing in the fellowship meals and the prayers (Acts 2:42). The fellowship meals were times when the believers would come together to eat and drink, with an opportunity to remember the death of Christ with bread and wine representing the body and blood of Christ. Today the church has the Communion or the Breaking of Bread service to remember what Jesus did for us on the cross. The church is the community of believers in togetherness and friendship.

The early church continued together in close fellowship and shared their belongings with one another. They would sell property and possessions and give the money to the apostles to distribute among those in the church who were in need (Acts 2:44). The church must be a sharing people who demonstrate practical love for one another.

Prayer

There is power in prayer. The early church devoted themselves to prayer and praise in public places and in their homes (Acts 2:42-47). Prayer is simply speaking to and listening to God. Prayer includes praise, thanks and biblical meditation - reading and thinking about the word of God. The Bible is necessary if we are to be thoroughly equipped in life, for all situations and good works. God is holy and so prayer includes confession of sin. God is our heavenly Father, once we have believed in and received Jesus into our lives (John 1:12-13). We can tell him about our needs and ask for his help. Prayer includes praying for others. God loves the world and so must we. Often we are prompted not only to pray but to help in practical ways.

The Bible

We receive teaching from the Bible, church meetings and Christians. It is a big advantage to have a healthy and positive attitude when we hear the word of God taught.

Read, reflect and apply the word. Discipline yourself to set aside time to do this. Blessed is the person whose delight is in the word of God and meditates on it often. That person will become like a tree planted by streams of water which produces fruit at the right time. Its leaves will not dry up, These people will succeed in everything they do (Psalm 1).

New Christians will benefit greatly from reading and reflecting on the accounts of Jesus found in the gospels. Start by reading Mark's Gospel straight through in just a few sittings. Then go back to the beginning and read a small section at a time. Think and reflect. Take your time. Enjoy it. Let it touch your heart. Let it speak. Spend months on this gospel. Ask yourself after each small section, 'What did Jesus say? What did he do?' Look at his compassion. Is there a promise to claim? Allow him to speak to you. Get to know Christ.

Sometimes the most simple thing will bless your heart. To the blind beggar Jesus said, 'What do you want me to do for you?' (Mark 10:46-52). Jesus asks you the same question today. In this story of the healing of blind Bartimaeus these words speak to me more than anything else about the compassion of Christ. Jesus was walking with a large crowd when Bartimaeus cried out. Some of the crowd told Bartimaeus to be quiet but Jesus stopped said, 'Call him.' Today Jesus stops for you. He will not ignore you or pass you by.

Chapter 3
PEACE AND POWER

Peace and power is available to all who follow Christ through the Holy Spirit. The peace of God is far more wonderful than the human mind can understand. The world cannot give the peace of Christ.

The early church was transformed from defeat and fear into victorious and strong people. The same Holy Spirit is freely available to you, to fill your life with peace and power.

The Holy Spirit is a counsellor, comforter and divine helper. Jesus Christ promised his disciples that they would experience a baptism with the Holy Spirit. Jesus told them he was going away, back to God, but that he would give them the Holy Spirit. Jesus always addressed the Holy Spirit as him or he, never as it (John 14:15-17, 16:5-11).

The Holy Spirit is a very powerful person. He is not a force. The Holy Spirit has personality. He speaks, guides and can be grieved (Ephesians 4:30). Fellowship and friendship with the Holy Spirit are encouraged (Philippians 2:1). Paul concludes his second letter to the church in Corinth by praying this prayer for them: 'May the grace of the Lord Jesus Christ, and the love of God and the fellowship of the Holy Spirit be with you all' (2 Corinthians 13:14).

Jesus told Nicodemus that he must be born again if he was to enter the kingdom of God - born again of the Holy Spirit (John 3:1-8). Jesus explained to Nicodemus that as he had experienced a physical birth, so he must have a spiritual birth through the Holy Spirit.

The Holy Spirit is the Spirit of truth. The Holy Spirit is the Spirit of Jesus, that is, he is the same in character as Jesus. The Holy Spirit is the third person of the Trinity. There is only one God. God-the-Father, God-the-Son (that is, Jesus), and God-the-Holy Spirit; three distinct persons.

When the Holy Spirit controls the life of the believer he produces these qualities: love, joy, peace, patience, kindness, goodness, faithfulness, gentleness, and self-control (Galatians 5:22-23). The Holy Spirit gives gifts to Christians as and when he decides, as we earnestly desire him and have fellowship with him. He gives wisdom, knowledge, faith, healings, miraculous powers, prophecy, the ability to distinguish between spirits, speaking in tongues, and the interpretation of tongues (1 Corinthians 12:7-10).

The Holy Spirit and Jesus

Jesus was anointed of the Holy Spirit. He was able to heal, deliver people from evil spirits, do the miraculous, teach and preach powerfully bringing help and relief. Jesus walked and talked with the Holy Spirit. Jesus did amazing things because of the Holy Spirit's power in and through him.

The fellowship of the Holy Spirit be with you.

John the Baptist appeared to prepare the way for Jesus. John instructed people to repent and get ready for the coming of the Christ. John baptised those who repented in the River Jordan. The water signified being cleansed from sin and new life. John said this of Jesus:

'I baptise you with water. But one more powerful than I will come, the thongs of whose sandals I am not worthy to untie. He will baptise you with the Holy Spirit and with fire'(Luke 3:15-16).

Jesus experienced the tremendous power of the Holy Spirit. After the resurrection Jesus baptised others with the Holy Spirit and with fire.

John baptised Jesus in water. While Jesus was praying

the heavens opened and the Holy Spirit came down on him in the form of a dove. A voice came from heaven that said, 'You are my Son, whom I love; with you I am well pleased' (Luke 3:21-22).

Jesus returned from the Jordan full of the Holy Spirit. He was led into the desert by the Holy Spirit. There he was tempted by the devil for forty days (Luke 4:1-2). Jesus went to Galilee in the power of the Spirit. The whole countryside heard about Jesus. He travelled around, teaching in the synagogues. Everyone praised him (Luke 4:14-19). He went to Nazareth, the town where he had grown up. On the Sabbath he went to the synagogue. The scroll of the prophet Isaiah was handed to him. He carefully unrolled it and found the place where it said:

'The Spirit of the Lord is on me, because he has anointed me to preach good news to the poor. He has sent me to proclaim freedom for the prisoners and recovery of sight for the blind, to release the oppressed, to proclaim the year of the Lord's favour' (Luke 4:17-19).

He rolled up the scroll, gave it back to the attendant and sat down. Everyone looked at him, waiting and wondering. Jesus said to them, 'Today this scripture is fulfilled in your hearing.'

Jesus announced that he was going to fulfil these things. He was going to bring healing, deliverance and salvation. Jesus did just that. Throughout his life and ministry the Spirit of God was on him. He was anointed by the Holy Spirit. Jesus drove out evil spirits from people (Luke 4:31-37; 8:26-39; 9:37-45; 11:14-28). He healed many (Luke 4:38-40). He healed those with leprosy (Luke 5:12-16). He healed a paralytic (Luke 5:17-26). He healed the centurion's dying servant (Luke 7:1-10). He raised a widow's son back to life (Luke 7:11-17). He raised a dead girl to life and healed a sick woman

(Luke 8:40-56). Jesus multiplied a few loaves and fish to feed 5,000 hungry men, plus women and children (Luke 9:10-17). He healed ten lepers (Luke 17:11-19).

Jesus' teaching on the Holy Spirit

One day one of Jesus' disciples asked him if he would teach them how to pray. Jesus taught them the Lord's prayer. He told them to ask, seek and knock, emphasising that they were to persevere in prayer. To finish he said these words:

> 'Which of you fathers, if your son asks for a fish, will give him a snake instead? Or if he asks for an egg, will give him a scorpion? If you then, though you are evil, know how to give good gifts to your children, how much more will your Father in heaven give the Holy Spirit to those who ask Him!' (Luke 11:11-13).

Jesus told his disciples that his Father wanted to give them the Holy Spirit - a good gift - to all those who ask. There is no question whether God will or will not give the Holy Spirit. The Counsellor, who is our helper and comforter, is available to us. He will teach us all things and will remind us of the words of Jesus. He will empower us.

The Holy Spirit comes

After his resurrection Jesus told his disciples to wait in Jerusalem until the Holy Spirit came on them. He made it clear that they were not to take the gospel to anyone until they had received the baptism with the Holy Spirit (Luke 24:45-49, Acts 1:7-8). They waited for the Holy Spirit.

When the Holy Spirit came, it was the Jewish feast of Pentecost, and the disciples were all together. Suddenly a sound like a violent wind came from heaven and filled the house. They saw what seemed to be tongues of fire that separated and came to rest on each of them. Each of them was baptised or filled with the Holy Spirit and spoke with other languages or tongues, as the Spirit enabled them (Acts 2:1-4).

A large crowd had gathered to see what the noise and excitement were about. Peter spoke to them about Jesus. Around 3,000 people heard his message, repented of their sins and were baptised in water. These new believers joined the church. The difference that the outpouring of the Holy Spirit made on the disciples in the upper room was obvious. They now had the power to witness effectively, just as Jesus had said.

The baptism with the Holy Spirit is given to equip Christians with boldness and power to share Christ.

The Holy Spirit and me

Immediately after becoming a Christian I attended an excellent youth fellowship. The Saturday sports and games evenings were most enjoyable. The Sunday evening meetings were extremely helpful to me as a young Christian. The speakers, Bible studies, worship and prayer times were instrumental in my formation as a follower of Jesus. I made new friends. Roger and Katie, our youth leaders, became my spiritual parents. They were people I could trust. They helped me to know Christ better.

After attending for six months they organised a holiday in the country for the group. It was a wonderful opportunity to get to know others, have fun and enjoy the Lord's presence. I did not know that something significant was going to happen to me during this time away. The theme of the week was 'The Holy Spirit in the life of the believer'. I asked the guest speakers about the baptism of the Holy Spirit. They suggested I went away and ask God to baptise me with his Holy Spirit. They promised they would pray for me too.

I prayed for the next two days. I remember being apart from the others to pray. I sensed that something was about to happen. I sat on top of a hill praying. As I looked down at the trees, fields and river at the bottom of the hill, I was praying for the baptism with the Holy Spirit. One night we returned to our dormitories to sleep. As I lay on the top bunk I asked God again to give me the baptism with the Holy Spirit and to change me. As I lay praying, joy came pouring into me, a joy that I had never experienced before. I experienced the love of Christ. I felt Christ's love. The joy was so great that I could not sleep. I asked God to take some of the joy away so that I could sleep. I finally fell asleep. That night God baptised me in his Holy Spirit.

The next day I told my youth leaders what had happened. They were delighted. There was an immediate difference in my life. I had an overwhelming desire and ability to share the Good News of Jesus and my story of knowing Christ with others. I shared with friends and strangers. I now had a power and boldness to witness effectively. There were several people that I had known for a long time who became Christians and started to go to church through my witness. I felt the Lord closer to me than ever before. The Bible had greater meaning and was increasingly relevant. I enjoyed praying immensely. For me, Christianity is about knowing Christ and making him known. Since my baptism with the Holy Spirit making him known has been a privilege and challenge.

How to be filled with the Holy Spirit

The Lord desires to baptise you in his Holy Spirit, that is to completely immerse you in his Spirit. Jesus is the baptiser (John 1:33) and he is with you right now. The Holy Spirit is a holy being. The Spirit will not settle in a sinful life. He is sensitive. Heavenly waters will not flow through polluted channels. So it is necessary for you to take the first step and confess and turn away from any wrong doing. In the early church the Spirit was given to all who obeyed (Acts 5:32).

> **You do not need to persuade Jesus to be kind to you and baptise you with his Holy Spirit and fire. He has already promised.**

Secondly, you must ask. Jesus said the Holy Spirit is given easily to those who simply ask (Luke 11:13). Jesus described the Holy Spirit to the woman at the well as living water and invited her to just ask for this gift of God (John 4:10). Will you ask?

The last step is to believe in Christ and his promise,

'If anyone is thirsty, let him come to me and drink. Whoever believes in me, as the Scripture has said, streams of living water will flow from within him' (John 7:37).

By this he meant the Holy Spirit who is available to you today. To come to Jesus begging and pleading is not necessary. Faith involves taking. It is a gift - take it. You do not need to persuade Jesus to be kind to you and baptise you with his Holy Spirit and fire. He has already promised. Come with boldness to collect what he offers you. It is a gift, so you must believe the giver, before you reach out to receive what he offers you.

God offers his Spirit. On Pentecost Peter said,

'The promise is for you and your children and for all who are far off - for all whom the Lord our God will call' (Acts 2:39).

For many people the baptism with the Holy Spirit comes

after becoming a Christian (Acts 8:15-16; 19:1-7). For some, conversion and the baptism in the Holy Spirit happen at the same time.

You need not wait for a special service. Remember to repent of any wrong ways and confess any sin. Ask and believe now. Find a place where you can pray, or ask a Christian friend to help you to pray a prayer like this:

> *Lord Jesus, I thank you for dying on the cross for me. I give my life totally to you today. I ask you to forgive my sin* (mention particular things). *I renounce completely my involvement in ...* (let the Holy Spirit bring things to mind). *I ask you now to give me your gift and baptise me with the Holy Spirit. I receive you now Holy Spirit. Come Holy Spirit. You are welcome. In the name of Jesus Christ. Amen.*

Spend a little time in quiet prayer, thanking God for his grace and goodness. Open your hands in a gesture of receiving. If you have asked and believed, God will keep his promise. We only receive the baptism in the Holy Spirit once, for all time. However, we need to ask God to fill us with his Holy Spirit over and over again, everyday, as we face certain situations and tasks. The formula is simple: one baptism, many fillings, constant anointing. The reason God anoints you is because he has other people in mind. May God bless you abundantly, as you discover for yourself the beauty and grace of the Holy Spirit.

Chapter 4

MAKING A DIFFERENCE

You are unique

There is no one like you. You are one of a kind. You were born an original. There is only one of you and you are unique and special. We seem to be able to believe that God loves us, but not believe that he likes us. God does like us. We need to accept that he likes us and learn to like ourselves.

When a visiting speaker came to our church one Sunday evening, it turned out to be very special. The praise that evening was especially exuberant. It was truly a celebration. Throughout the evening I was feeling expectant that something would happen. I was praying that the preacher would prophesy the word of the Lord to me. I knew that this person had been used in this way before. It was almost as if I knew he would. I was full of hope.

When he finished speaking he pointed to four individuals in turn and spoke an encouraging, comforting and strengthening word to each. Gerald Coates spoke clearly, publicly for all to hear. He spoke to me saying that in the future doors would be open for me to speak internationally. He said that God would use my charismatic personality and gifting. He said that there would be occasions when the gift of prophecy would flow through me. People in church that evening were excited for us. I received the word that Gerald had given. I weighed it up and believed it to be true. I kept it in my heart and waited for it to be fulfilled and tried to meet the conditions attached to it. The word was from the Lord through one of his servants.

Something similar happened in the life of Nathanael:

When Jesus saw Nathanael approaching, he said of him, 'Here is a true Israelite, in whom there is nothing false.'

'How do you know me?' Nathanael asked.

Jesus answered, 'I saw you while you were still under the fig tree before Philip called you.'

Then Nathanael declared 'Rabbi, you are the Son of God; you are the King of Israel.'

Jesus said, 'You believe because I told you I saw you under the fig tree. You shall see greater things than that.' He then added, 'I tell you the truth, you shall see heaven open, and the angels of God ascending and descending on the Son of Man' (John 1:47-51).

Three months later I attended the annual evangelists' conference in Swanwick, England. During one meeting we got into small groups to pray together. Our group had just finished, others were still praying. A woman approached me and quietly said, 'I believe I have a word for you from the Lord. Can I tell you it?' At once I recognised her voice and knew her to be Jean Darnell. The essence of what she said was this:

> I see you with a microphone in one hand and a notebook in the other. From your notebook you are preaching other people's words and sermons. Put the notebook away. You are unique and original. Again, I see you on a platform with your Bible in one hand and a microphone in the other. You are speaking powerfully God's word with the Bible to thousands. You are unique and original. Be so.

Somehow, by the gift of the Holy Spirit given to her, Jean Darnell knew something of my past, what I was like, and predicted something about my future. Concerning the future - it came true. It was true that I had been using other preachers' sermons. The emphasis on being unique and original was helpful and challenging for my formation. The part about speaking to large crowds with only my Bible and a microphone was to be fulfilled sooner than I knew.

A few weeks afterwards, Korky Davey, a wonderful evangelist and facilitator of others, invited me to be part of his team on a trip to Nigeria. This was the most amazing and challenging time of my life. On the first Sunday of our trip, we were seated with the other leaders at the front of the church. There were thousands of people in front of us. Korky turned quietly and informed me that I was to speak. I was not prepared. Many thoughts rushed through my mind. My little sermon outline book was with me. I spoke to the best of my ability but I felt hindered, not liberated. I was not entirely happy. Why? I was tied down to notes. I had not learnt to be myself - unique and original as Jean Darnell had said.

There is no-one like you. You are one of a kind. You were born an original.

For the first few days I took the little sermon outline book with me, but it did not help. The word given to me by Jean Darnell was for now and it came to mind vividly. I made the decision to leave behind the outline book. It was time to be original and unique, to depend on God and myself.

Each time I was asked to preach I spoke with only my Bible in hand. I spoke with passion from my heart. This was a new beginning for me. There would be more visits to other nations in Africa and Europe. On every occasion I would speak with the Bible in hand. I had learnt a valuable lesson; God has made me unique and original. There is no need to try and be someone else. The text-book definition of preaching is: 'God speaking through personality.'

You too are unique. We are born original, but the majority of people die as copies. With the gifts that God gives you, you can make a difference to your family, friends, your church, and the world.

You Are talented

There was a certain man about to go on a journey (Matthew 25:14-30). He called his servants and put them in charge of his property. He gave to each one according to his ability. One servant received five talents, another two and another one. This parable that Jesus told has vital lessons for us today.

A 'talent' was a unit of coinage. One talent was the same as 1,000 gold coins. The talents were entrusted to the three servants and it was their responsibility and opportunity to make money for their master. The servant who had five talents put his money to work and earned five more. Similarly the servant who had two talents earned two more. But the servant who had been given one talent dug a hole in the ground and hid it.

After a long time the master returned and settled accounts with them. He congratulated the first two servants and rewarded them with gifts because of their faithfulness in managing what they had been given. The servant who was given one talent tried to justify himself by saying, 'Master I knew that you are a hard man, harvesting where you have not sown and gathering where you have not scattered seed. So I was afraid and went out and hid your talent in the ground. See, here is what belongs to you.'

The master was not pleased with this and told his servant that he was lazy and bad. He asked him why he did not put the talent to some use by placing it in the bank to earn interest. The one talent was removed from the servant and given to the one who had ten. Jesus concluded the parable by saying:

'For everyone who has will be given more, and he will have an abundance. Whoever does not have, even what he has will be taken from him. And throw that worthless servant outside, into darkness, where there will be weeping and gnashing of teeth' (Matthew 25:29-30).

There are three important principles to note here:

Each and every Christian is given a gift. Jesus uses the term talent to indicate an ability or gift given to an individual. God has given us time, gifts and other resources. He expects us to put them to good use. No one is excluded. Jesus, like the master in the parable, is wise and discerning to know what to give. No Christian receives more or less than he or she can handle. If we fail in our task our excuse can not be that we are overwhelmed. The lack of success may be because of laziness or disobedience.

Fear can stop us. The servant said to the master, 'So I was afraid and went out and hid your talent in the ground'. Fear prevented the servant using the talent he was given. He was obsessed with safety and security. Do not bury your talent. Use your God-given gifts to advance the kingdom of God and to do good. Do not be afraid. Many Christians have stopped or have not started to use their gifts or talents. Our time, abilities or money are not ours - we are caretakers. Christians must not ignore, squander or abuse what they have; inaction for whatever reason in inappropriate.

The tragedy of life is not being limited to one talent but failing to use the one talent.

A wrong view of someone or something can hinder us. The servant had a wrong view of and relationship with his master. 'Master, I knew that you are a hard man...' (Matthew 25:24). This perception, together with the fear, prevented the servant from using his talent. There are those who have a poor and inadequate relationship with God. This does not have to be. For Christians God is Abba - Father. He is compassionate and loving towards his children. The kind of fear we should have of God is one of respect and honour, not a dreadful terrifying fear. The servant would have done better if his beliefs and relationship with his master were like that described here:

> The Lord is compassionate and gracious, slow to anger, abounding in love. He will not always accuse, nor will he harbour his anger for ever; he does not treat us as our sins deserve or repay us according to our iniquities. For as high as the heavens are above the earth, so great is his love for those who fear him (Psalm 103:8-11).

Whether you are a five, two or one talent person does not matter. You are gifted. The tragedy of life is not being limited to one talent, but failing to use the one talent. You can make a difference.

Spiritual gifts

Jesus operated in the power of the Holy Spirit. He was endowed with spiritual gifts. The four gospels clearly show that his three years of public ministry included healings, miracles, deliverance, and prophecy. Many people were set free and given a new start because of the manifestation of the Holy Spirit working through him. The Apostle Paul was also able to heal and save because he allowed the spiritual gifts to flow through him. Paul encouraged believers to do the same in order that the church would be built up and made stronger. Paul instructed the church at Corinth to follow the way of love and eagerly desire the spiritual gifts (see 1 Corinthians 12:31; 14:1).

For the good of all

There are different kinds of gifts. There are gifts of wisdom, knowledge, faith, healing, miracles, prophecy, discernment or distinguishing between spirits, speaking in different kinds of tongues, and the interpretation of tongues (1 Corinthians 12:8-10). The Holy Spirit gives these spiritual gifts to each one, as he determines, for the common good (1 Corinthians 12:4-7).

You can make a difference.

Believers must pursue the way of love and eagerly desire the spiritual gifts if these manifestations are to occur in us and through us to others. Paul says to the Christians in Corinth, 'Since you are eager to have spiritual gifts, try to excel in gifts that build up the church' (1 Corinthians 14:12).

Again and again Paul spells out that the edification, strengthening and encouragement of the church is of great importance in the exercise of the spiritual gifts (1 Corinthians 14:4-5; 12-17; 26-31).

In addition to these gifts of the Holy Spirit there are the gifts of Christ. Apostles, prophets, evangelists, pastors and teachers exist to equip the church for service and to build up the church (Ephesians 4:11-13).

The seven gifts of God are listed by Paul: prophecy, serving, teaching, encouraging, giving (to the need of others), leadership, and showing mercy (Romans 12:6-8).

Indispensable people

Paul likens the church to the human body. The church has many parts, with Christ as its head. The body is not made up of only one part, but of many parts.

There are Christians who despise themselves. They say that they do not belong to the rest of the church - the body of believers - because they are not like somebody else: 'Because I am not a hand I do not belong to the body' (1 Corinthians 12:15).

This is unnecessary and unhelpful. It is self-persecution. Unfortunately there are also those within the church who reject their brothers or sisters by saying they are not needed: 'The eye cannot say to the hand, "I do not need you!"' (1 Corinthians 12:21).

A myth exists. I have heard it said that no one is indispensable. The Bible says the opposite. Paul dispels the myth and puts the record straight when he says, 'On the contrary, those parts of the body that seem to be weaker are indispensable' (1 Corinthians 12:22).

There are those in churches who are of paramount importance. Do not be surprised that these are the weaker members. They are important to God, his church and his kingdom. We cannot do without the weaker members. They are indispensable. The Bible says so. Paul goes on to say that the parts that we think are less honourable or not worth much we should treat with special honour. The parts that are unpresentable or obscure should be treated with special modesty.

You are gifted. What is your gift and contribution? You can make a difference.

Christian giving

The early church was a caring and sharing community. The church in Jerusalem was over 3,000 strong. The Christians spent their time learning from the Apostles and taking part in the fellowship. They shared meals and broke bread, remembering the death of Christ. They were committed to prayer and to each other. The Apostles performed miracles and wonders in the name of Jesus by the power of the Holy Spirit. The believers continued together in close fellowship and shared their belongings: 'selling their possessions and goods, they gave to anyone as he had need' (Acts 2:45).

As time went on the church continued to be a loving fellowship. The believers were of one heart and mind. The Christians did not claim that their possessions were their own to hold on to, but they shared with anyone who had need. There were no needy people in the church because from time to time those who owned fields or houses would sell them and donate the money from the sale to the Apostles. This was then distributed to each according to their need (Acts 4:32-35). This amazing behaviour was voluntary. It did not involve all private property, only that which was needed. It was not a condition of membership into the church.

It is our responsibility and privilege to help those who are destitute, poor or needy.

What we give is very much up to us. There is great need in the world and the church. God has a bias toward the poor and needy. It is our responsibility and privilege to help those who are destitute, poor or needy. The early church was extremely generous. We also need to have open hearts and pockets to do whatever we can.

Paul's words to the Christians in the early church concerning giving are helpful guidance for us today. He encouraged generous giving within their means, for he did not want those who gave to place themselves in distress.

> ... Give whatever you can according to what you have. If you are really eager to give, it isn't important how much you are able to give. God wants you to give what you have, not what you don't have. Of course, I don't mean you should give so much that you suffer from having too little. I only mean that there should be some equality.
> (2 Corinthians 8:11-13 NLT)

We must be open to the Lord and what he would say to us. A man stood up in a Christian meeting in London and publicly said that he was going to stop his monthly giving to the leisure club and give instead to the needs of his people in Nigeria. This man was faithful to his word and has since helped to sponsor needy children through school in Africa.

A few weeks after I had preached at a church our

organisation received a generous cheque from a dear elderly woman who said the Lord told her to give it.

While in Africa I felt I should give a donation to all the staff at a Christian College, knowing that doing so would mean that our organisation would not have sufficient funds to pay my salary on time that month. We must let our hearts be touched.

As a family we give each month to our local church and to a full time evangelist. We also support causes and individuals from time to time.

I have seen great poverty in Africa. Despite this the Christians there give generously. For them giving to God's work is as important as worshipping God - it is part of their worship. Several collections in one meeting are common. There is joy on their faces as they give. In such places revival has occurred and continues. Let us be generous.

ABOUT THE AUTHOR

Andy Economides' work and passion is to spread the Good News of Jesus and bring people to know and follow Christ, throughout the UK and in other countries. Particular emphasis is given to the nurture of new believers and the training of leaders and churches. Andy is Patron of Prospect College and School, Nigeria, West Africa. Through his fund-raising a new school has been established and the college extended. Scholarships for college students and sponsorships for children are provided through Soteria Trust.

Andy originally qualified as an engineer and worked for six years in research and development. For ten years he was on the staff of a church as a lay minister and evangelist. In 1989 St John's Theological College, Nottingham, awarded Andy the College Hood for Theological and Pastoral Studies. In 1994 Andy became founder and director of Soteria Trust, a registered charity. The word *Soteria* is Greek for 'salvation'. Reverend Andy Economides was ordained as a Christian minister in 1998.

If you would like to know more about the ministry of Andy Economides through Soteria Trust, or would like to order books and resources, please complete the response slip and send it to:

SOTERIA TRUST
PO BOX 103 CHICHESTER PO19 2XY UK

Tele: 01243 771494 **Fax:** 01243 771240
E-mail: admin@soteriatrust.org.uk
Website: www.soteriatrust.org.uk
Registered Charity No: 1040766

RESPONSE SLIP

Please send me:

☐ The *Soteria News* regularly

☐ Information about books and tapes available

☐ Information about how I can be involved

I enclose a gift of £ ....…….. towards the ministry of Soteria Trust. (Please make all cheques payable to *Soteria Trust*).

Name ....

Address ....

....

.... Post Code ....

E-mail ....